FIREFLY BOOKS

A FIREFLY BOOK

Published by Firefly Books Ltd. 2014

Second printing

Publisher Cataloging-in-Publication Data (U.S.)
A CIP record for this title is available from the Library of Congress

Library and Archives Canada Cataloguing in Publication
A CIP record for this title is available from Library and Archives Canada

Published in the United States by
Firefly Books (U.S.) Inc.
P.O. Box 1338, Ellicott Station
Buffalo, New York 14205

Published in Canada by
Firefly Books Ltd.
50 Staples Avenue, Unit 1
Richmond Hill, Ontario L4B 0A7

Cover and interior design: Kimberley Young
Illustrations: George Todorovic
Creative Direction: Steve Cameron

Printed in China

The publisher gratefully acknowledges the financial support for our publishing program
by the Government of Canada through the Canada Book Fund as administered by
the Department of Canadian Heritage.

CONTENTS

PLUS

SIDNEY CROSBY, STEVEN STAMKOS,
ALEX OVECHKIN, HENRIK SEDIN,
DANIEL SEDIN, JOHN TAVARES,
JAROME IGINLA, JONATHAN TOEWS,
ANZE KOPITAR, PATRICK KANE,
EVGENI MALKIN AND MANY MORE!

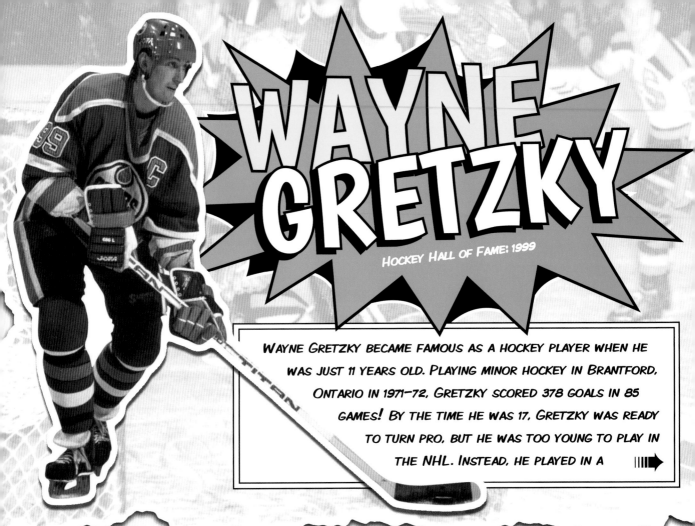

WAYNE GRETZKY

HOCKEY HALL OF FAME: 1999

WAYNE GRETZKY BECAME FAMOUS AS A HOCKEY PLAYER WHEN HE WAS JUST 11 YEARS OLD. PLAYING MINOR HOCKEY IN BRANTFORD, ONTARIO IN 1971–72, GRETZKY SCORED 378 GOALS IN 85 GAMES! BY THE TIME HE WAS 17, GRETZKY WAS READY TO TURN PRO, BUT HE WAS TOO YOUNG TO PLAY IN THE NHL. INSTEAD, HE PLAYED IN A ▮▮▮➤

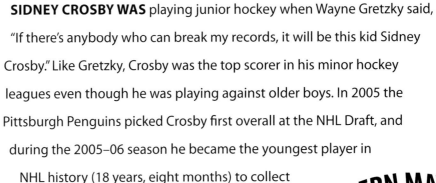

SIDNEY CROSBY WAS playing junior hockey when Wayne Gretzky said, "If there's anybody who can break my records, it will be this kid Sidney Crosby." Like Gretzky, Crosby was the top scorer in his minor hockey leagues even though he was playing against older boys. In 2005 the Pittsburgh Penguins picked Crosby first overall at the NHL Draft, and during the 2005–06 season he became the youngest player in NHL history (18 years, eight months) to collect 100 points. He was still just 19 years old when he won his first NHL scoring title in 2006–07.

MODERN MATCH
SIDNEY CROSBY

rival league called the World Hockey Association (WHA). Gretzky joined the Edmonton Oilers that year, and even though he was playing against men twice his age, he finished the 1978–79 WHA season third in the league with 110 points.

Before the start of the 1979–80 season, the Oilers joined the NHL and nobody thought Gretzky would succeed. He was a small and skinny kid, and he didn't look like a hockey star. Yet Gretzky made up for his lack of size with his amazing awareness on the ice. Gretzky could spot patterns in the game and find open teammates to create plays that others didn't see. He collected 51 goals and 86 assists for 137 points during his first NHL season. A year later, he broke the NHL record of 152 points when he got 164. And the year after that Gretzky scored 92 goals in one season to smash the old record of 76. In 1985–86, he broke his own records when he set new NHL marks with 163 assists and 215 points!

In just his 11th NHL season, Gretzky scored the 1,851st point of his career. His childhood hero Gordie Howe previously held the record of 1,850 points, and it took him 26 years to set it! Gretzky would later break Howe's record of 801 goals as well, finishing his NHL career with 894 goals and 1,963 assists for 2,857 points — the most in NHL history!

Did You Know?

WAYNE GRETZKY WON THE ART ROSS TROPHY AS NHL SCORING LEADER A RECORD 10 TIMES IN HIS 20-YEAR CAREER.

Blast FROM THE Past — JOE MALONE (HHOF: 1950)

Hockey was very different when Joe Malone played over 100 years ago. Forward passing wasn't allowed, so players had to be great puckhandlers. Teams also only carried a few substitutes, meaning the best players often played the whole game and got plenty of chances to score goals. However, very few outscored Joe Malone. During the NHL's first season of 1917–18, Malone netted a league-leading 44 goals for the Montreal Canadiens. He did it in just 20 games! Playing for the Quebec Bulldogs on January 31, 1920, Malone scored seven goals in one game, still an NHL record.

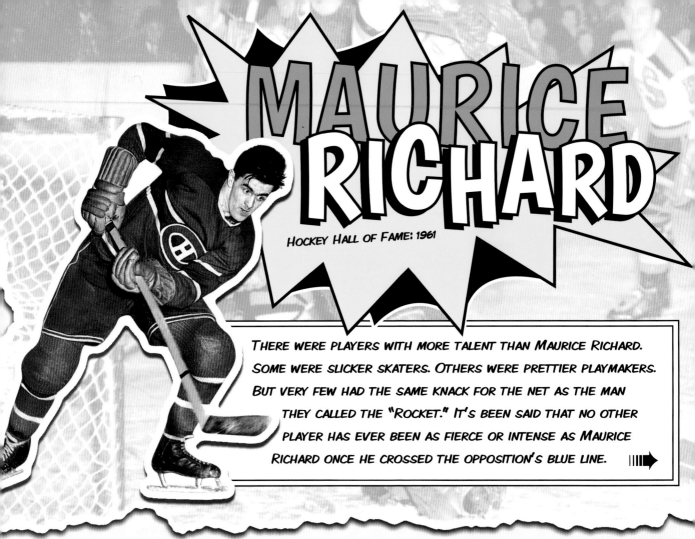

MAURICE RICHARD

HOCKEY HALL OF FAME: 1961

THERE WERE PLAYERS WITH MORE TALENT THAN MAURICE RICHARD. SOME WERE SLICKER SKATERS. OTHERS WERE PRETTIER PLAYMAKERS. BUT VERY FEW HAD THE SAME KNACK FOR THE NET AS THE MAN THEY CALLED THE "ROCKET." IT'S BEEN SAID THAT NO OTHER PLAYER HAS EVER BEEN AS FIERCE OR INTENSE AS MAURICE RICHARD ONCE HE CROSSED THE OPPOSITION'S BLUE LINE. ▐▐▐➡

He didn't have Maurice Richard's intensity, but Pavel "The Russian Rocket" Bure had speed to burn. He also had incredible balance, which made him hard to knock off the puck. And when he got the puck near the net, he knew what to do with it! Bure began his NHL career with the Vancouver Canucks in 1991–92. No Vancouver player had ever scored 50 goals, but in 1992–93 Bure scored 60! He did it again the following year. Later, with the Florida Panthers, Bure had two more 50-plus-goal seasons. He scored 437 career goals before injuries forced him to retire.

THE RUSSIAN ROCKET

HOCKEY HALL OF FAME: 2012

Pavel BURE

Richard was born and raised in a working-class section of Montreal. When he was starring with the hometown Canadiens in the 1940s and 1950s, many French-Canadian families were struggling to make a living (even in Quebec), and they loved to watch Richard dominate the mostly English-speaking game. Other players often picked on him, breaking the rules to try to slow him down. Many times, Richard fought back, and sometimes his fiery temper got him into trouble. Still, Richard was the heart and soul of the Montreal Canadiens. He played with the team for 18 years from 1942 to 1960 and helped them win the Stanley Cup eight times!

Richard burst out as a star during his second season with the Canadiens in 1943–44. He ranked among the league leaders with 32 goals during the regular season. Then, in the playoffs, he scored 12 more to lead Montreal to the Stanley Cup. A year later, Richard became the first player in NHL history to score 50 goals in a season, and the season was only 50 games long! It was the first of five times that Richard led the NHL in goals. He went on to become the first NHL player to score 500 career goals. No wonder the NHL awards the Maurice "Rocket" Richard Trophy to the league's top goal scorer.

Blast FROM THE Past   NEWSY LALONDE (HHOF: 1950)

There's a famous saying written on the wall of the Montreal Canadiens dressing room. It's from the World War I poem *In Flanders Field*: "To you from failing hands we throw the torch, be yours to hold it high." It means that as one generation gets old, the traditions are passed on to the next. The tradition of Montreal's great scoring stars begins with Newsy Lalonde, who joined the Canadiens in their first season of 1909–10, seven years before the NHL began. He retired with 440 career goals, and the next closest player was Joe Malone, far behind with 337.

MIKE BOSSY

Hockey Hall of Fame: 1991

According to family stories, Mike Bossy's father gave him a plastic hockey stick when Bossy was just two years old. He wanted to see what might happen. What happened was his son grew up to be one of the greatest scorers in hockey history! ▐▐▶

Dynamite Linemates

Bryan Trottier (HHOF: 1997)	Clarke Gillies (HHOF: 2002)

At his first training camp with the New York Islanders, Mike Bossy was placed on a line with Bryan Trottier and Clarke Gillies. Trottier had been the rookie of the year in 1974–75. He was a great playmaker who could score goals too. Gillies was a tough customer who could score as well as hit. Together, they were almost unstoppable! The line was known as the "Trio Grande" but was sometimes called the Long Island Electric Company or the Long Island Lighting Company because of the offensive power they supplied.

From the time he started playing hockey, Mike Bossy could always score. In junior hockey, he set a record with 309 goals in just over four seasons. That's an average of nearly 78 goals per year! The Quebec junior league was a rough one, and Bossy hated the violence. He didn't like to fight. Instead, he believed: "If you knock me down, I will get back up and score more goals." Even so, many NHL scouts thought that Bossy wasn't tough enough. It took until the 15th pick in the 1977 NHL Draft before the New York Islanders chose him. Bossy made the team right away, and during the 1977–78 season he became the first rookie in NHL history to score 50 goals! The next year, Bossy led the league with 69 goals. In 1979–80, he helped the Islanders win their first of four straight Stanley Cups!

Heading into the 1980–81 season, Bossy quietly set a challenge for himself. Twenty-three different players had scored 50 goals in a season since Maurice Richard did it first in 1944–45. Still, no one had managed to score 50 goals in just 50 games as Richard had done. That's what Bossy set out to do. Through the first 49 games, he'd scored 48 goals, and with time running out in game number 50, Bossy scored twice in the final five minutes to reach 50 goals! In all, Bossy scored 50 goals a record nine consecutive times in his 10-year NHL career.

Did You Know?

MIKE BOSSY SCORED 573 GOALS IN JUST 752 GAMES. THAT'S AN NHL RECORD SCORING AVERAGE OF .762 GOALS-PER-GAME.

MODERN MATCH
STEVEN STAMKOS

THERE WAS NO waiting around on draft day for Steven Stamkos. Tampa Bay made the slick center the very first choice of the 2008 NHL Draft. He didn't quite have the same fast start as Mike Bossy, but his 23 goals in 2008–09 ranked him third among NHL rookies. In his second season of 2009–10, Stamkos tied Sidney Crosby for the NHL lead with 51 goals.

He alone led the league with 60 goals in 2011–12. Like Bossy, who could fire the puck the moment it reached his stick, Stamkos is known for his lightning-quick "one-timers."

GORDIE HOWE

HOCKEY HALL OF FAME: 1972

GORDIE HOWE, ALSO KNOWN AS "MR. HOCKEY," BEGAN HIS NHL CAREER WITH THE DETROIT RED WINGS IN 1946. HE ENDED IT ALMOST 40 YEARS LATER WITH THE HARTFORD WHALERS IN 1980! IN BETWEEN, HOWE SET RECORDS THAT ONCE SEEMED UNBREAKABLE. HIS NHL TOTALS OF 801 GOALS AND 1,049 ASSISTS FOR 1,850 POINTS ▐▐▐▶

FROM THE VAULT

GORDIE'S MITTS

Gordie Howe wore these gloves during the 1952–53 season. That year, he led the NHL with 49 goals. At the time, Maurice Richard was the only player in NHL history who had ever scored 50 goals in one season. Howe also led the NHL with 46 assists in 1952–53, giving him 95 points. That total broke the single-season record of 86 points Howe himself had set two years earlier! Howe also won the Hart Trophy as NHL MVP for the second year in a row in 1952–53.

have now been beaten, but his 1,767 games played remains the most in NHL history.

Standing 6-feet tall (183 cm) and weighing 205 pounds (92 kg), Howe was one of the biggest and strongest players of his era. He wasn't dirty, but he was known for using his elbows to punish opponents that got too rough with him. Howe was also ambidextrous, meaning he could use both hands equally well. He generally shot right handed, but playing at a time when sticks had straight blades, he sometimes switched and shot left-handed to fool the goalie.

Howe started his NHL career slowly, but by his fourth year of 1949–50, he began a streak that saw him finish among the league's top-five scorers for 20 straight seasons! He won the scoring title and was named the league MVP six times each. He also helped Detroit win four Stanley Cups. Still going strong when he was 40 years old, Howe set a career-high with 103 points in 1968–69. He was just the third NHL player ever to reach the 100-point plateau. He still remains the oldest 100-point scorer in NHL history!

Howe retired in 1971 after 25 years with Detroit. Two years later, he made a comeback to play with his sons Mark and Marty in the World Hockey Association (WHA). After six years in the WHA, Howe returned to the NHL for a final season in 1979–80. He was 51 years old!

Did You Know?

GORDIE HOWE LED THE NHL IN SCORING FOUR YEARS IN A ROW FROM 1950–51 TO 1953–54.

Dynamite Linemates

SID ABEL (HHOF: 1969)	TED LINDSAY (HHOF: 1966)

Right winger Gordie Howe first lined up with center Sid Abel and left winger Ted Lindsay during the 1946–47 season. Soon they were the top line in hockey. Writers dubbed the trio "The Production Line" in 1948–49, and they produced plenty of points! Abel led the NHL in goals that year and won the Hart Trophy as league MVP. The next season, Lindsay led the league in scoring. Howe won his first scoring title the following year, making it three straight years the Production Line produced the top scorer in the NHL.

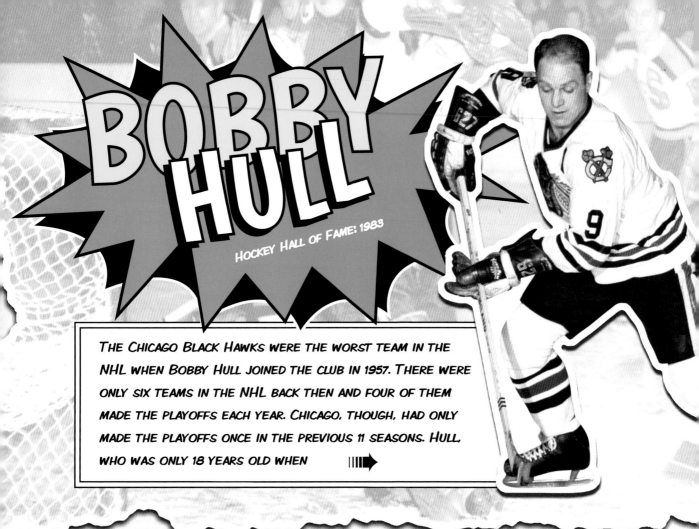

BOBBY HULL

Hockey Hall of Fame: 1983

THE CHICAGO BLACK HAWKS WERE THE WORST TEAM IN THE NHL WHEN BOBBY HULL JOINED THE CLUB IN 1957. THERE WERE ONLY SIX TEAMS IN THE NHL BACK THEN AND FOUR OF THEM MADE THE PLAYOFFS EACH YEAR. CHICAGO, THOUGH, HAD ONLY MADE THE PLAYOFFS ONCE IN THE PREVIOUS 11 SEASONS. HULL, WHO WAS ONLY 18 YEARS OLD WHEN ▐▐▶

THE CHICAGO BLACKHAWKS had missed the playoffs seven times in eight years when they chose Patrick Kane with the very first pick in the 2007 NHL Entry Draft. Kane made the team that year and won the Calder Trophy as the NHL's 2007–08 rookie of the year. Chicago still missed the playoffs, but thanks to Kane, and fellow rookie Jonathan Toews, the Hawks were improving. Just two years later, in 2009–10, the Blackhawks were Stanley Cup champions. Kane scored the Cup-winning goal in overtime to lead Chicago past Philadelphia in six games.

MODERN MATCH
PATRICK KANE

the 1957–58 season started, was the youngest player in the NHL. Chicago missed the playoffs again that year, but Hull and the Hawks were improving. By his third season of 1959–60, Hull was the top scorer in the NHL. One year later, the Black Hawks were Stanley Cup champions.

Hull was the most exciting scorer the NHL had seen in years. He was the fastest skater in the league and his huge, bulging biceps were bigger than the heavyweight boxing champions of the day. Hull used those powerful muscles — and a huge curve in the blade of his stick — to launch unbelievable slap shots. The tools used to measure the speed of shots weren't as good as they are today, but Hull's slapper was said to reach nearly 120 miles per hour (almost 200 kph)!

Maurice Richard became the first player

to score 50 goals in a season when he collected his 50th goal in the 50th and final game of the 1944–45 season. Even after the NHL extended the season to 70 games, only Montreal's Bernie Geoffrion, in 1960–61, was able to score 50 goals. But Bobby Hull became the league's third 50-goal man in 1961–62. In 1965–66, Hull set a new record with 54 goals. He upped that to 58 in 1968–69. That season also marked the seventh time that Hull was the NHL's top goal-scorer. That's a record nobody has beaten.

HOWIE MORENZ (HHOF: 1945) — Blast FROM THE Past

Bobby Hull's blazing speed was often compared to that of the speedy Howie Morenz, the NHL's top offensive star of the 1920s and early 1930s. Morenz joined the Montreal Canadiens for the 1923–24 season and promptly led them to the Stanley Cup. They won it again in 1929–30 and 1930–31. Morenz led the league in points twice and was the first player in history to win the Hart Trophy as MVP three times. Still, it was his speed that really wowed people. It earned him nicknames like the "Canadien Comet," the "Mitchell Meteor" and the "Stratford Streak."

BRETT HULL

Hockey Hall of Fame: 2009

It takes plenty of practice to make it to the NHL. It also helps if hockey talent runs in the family. There have been nearly 300 sets of brothers who've made it to the NHL, and more than 100 fathers and sons. Bobby Hull had a brother ▶▶▶

Dynamite Linemates

ADAM OATES (HHOF: 2012)

Adam Oates began his career in Detroit before joining Brett Hull in St. Louis in 1989–90. Hull needed someone to feed him the puck, and Oates was a brilliant playmaker. The two stars made an instant connection and rocketed up the scoring charts together! Hull and Oates were nearly unstoppable, and in a little less than three seasons in St. Louis the playmaker posted 228 assists! Traded to Boston, Oates led the NHL with 97 assists and posted career-best marks of 45 goals and 142 points in 1992–93.

named Dennis who scored 303 goals in his NHL career, but it was Bobby's son Brett who would join him in the Hockey Hall of Fame.

It was obvious that Brett Hull had heaps of talent. He piled up plenty of goals on his way to the NHL, but he didn't come across as a hard worker. Many hockey experts thought he was slow and lazy. Calgary picked him late in the 1984 NHL Draft, but barely played him before trading him to St. Louis. When Hull joined the Blues, everything suddenly came together. He scored 41 goals during

his first full season in St. Louis in 1988–89. The next year, he led the NHL with 72 goals. Hull led the league again in 1990–91. His 86 goals that year marked the third highest single-season total ever scored in the NHL! He won the Hart Trophy as the league's most valuable player, making him and Bobby the only father-and-son MVPs in NHL history. "The Golden Brett" led the league for the third straight year with 70 more goals in 1991–92. After leaving St. Louis in 1998, Hull won the Stanley Cup with Dallas and then Detroit.

Like his father Bobby, Brett Hull had a strong shot, but what made him so dangerous was his quick release. Brett had a knack for finding open spaces on the ice. Once he slipped into a gap, and a teammate passed him the puck, it was on its way to the net in a flash!

Did You Know?

BRETT HULL SCORED 741 GOALS DURING HIS 20 SEASONS IN THE NHL. THAT'S THE THIRD-HIGHEST TOTAL IN LEAGUE HISTORY.

BRETT'S BLUE THREADS

Brett Hull wore this jersey with the St. Louis Blues during the 1989–90 season. That year he led the league with 72 goals and became a superstar. It was the first of three straight seasons that Hull led the league in goals, and the first of five years in a row that he scored more than 50! Brett and Bobby Hull are the only father and son to have scored 50 goals in an NHL season. They're also the only ones to score 500 goals in their careers. In fact, they both scored more than 600!

FROM THE VAULT

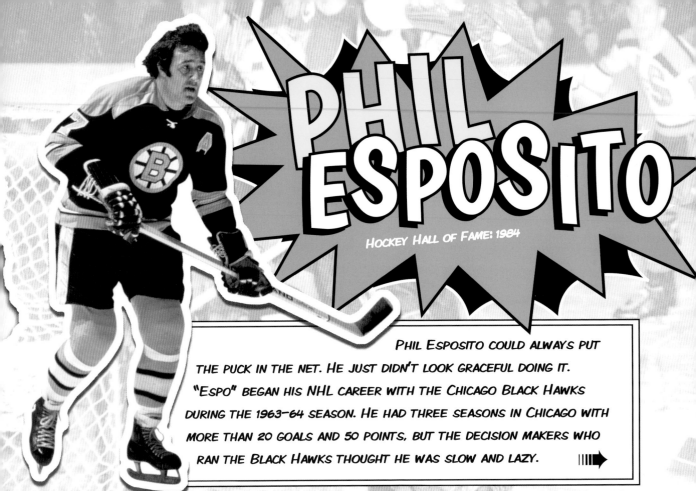

PHIL ESPOSITO

HOCKEY HALL OF FAME: 1984

PHIL ESPOSITO COULD ALWAYS PUT THE PUCK IN THE NET. HE JUST DIDN'T LOOK GRACEFUL DOING IT. "ESPO" BEGAN HIS NHL CAREER WITH THE CHICAGO BLACK HAWKS DURING THE 1963-64 SEASON. HE HAD THREE SEASONS IN CHICAGO WITH MORE THAN 20 GOALS AND 50 POINTS, BUT THE DECISION MAKERS WHO RAN THE BLACK HAWKS THOUGHT HE WAS SLOW AND LAZY. ||||➤

PHIL ESPOSITO SET an NHL record for shots on goal in a single season with 550 in 1970–71. Since then, only Alex Ovechkin has even come close to Esposito's record. Ovechkin broke into the NHL with a bang in 2005–06. He scored 52 goals that season and became the first rookie to lead the NHL in shots on goal. He went on to lead the league again for a record six straight seasons. In 2008–09 Ovechkin became just the second player in NHL history to top 500 shots when he led the league with 528!

MODERN MATCH
ALEX OVECHKIN

Little did they know that he would soon become an NHL superstar! In 1967, Chicago traded Esposito to Boston where he teamed with defenseman Bobby Orr to rewrite the NHL record book.

The Chicago bosses were right about one thing: Espo wasn't a great or fast skater. But he learned to succeed in other ways. Big and strong at 6-foot-1 (185 cm) and 205 pounds (92 kg), he played in front of the other team's net in the area known as "the slot." Standing there, Espo would take passes from his teammates and fire away. During the 1968–69 season, he became the first player in NHL history to top 100 points. He didn't just reach that milestone mark; he shattered it by registering 126 points. Then, in 1969–70, Esposito and Orr helped the Bruins win the Stanley Cup for the first time in 29 years!

Did You Know?

PHIL ESPOSITO WAS THE LEADING SCORER IN THE TOURNAMENT WHEN TEAM CANADA DEFEATED RUSSIA IN THE THRILLING 1972 SUMMIT SERIES.

Esposito had his greatest statistical season in 1970–71. The NHL record for goals in one season was 58, but Espo smashed that when he scored 76! He added 76 assists that year to set another new record with 152 points. He led the league in points again the next three seasons, and had the most goals for four straight years.

Hockey fans were shocked when the Bruins traded Esposito to New York in 1975. He finished out his career with the Rangers, retiring in 1981 with 717 goals.

Blast FROM THE Past   FRANK MCGEE (HHOF: 1945)

Frank McGee was a scoring sensation in the early 1900s. Seasons were short back then, but McGee didn't need a lot of games to pile up a ton of goals. He played only 45 games during four seasons with the Ottawa "Silver Seven" from 1902 to 1906, but scored more than 120 goals! McGee's most amazing feat came on January 16, 1905, when he scored 14 goals in a single Stanley Cup playoff game! Most amazing of all, McGee scored all those goals even though he was blind in one eye because of an injury.

MATS SUNDIN

Hockey Hall of Fame: 2012

MATS SUNDIN WAS THE FIRST EUROPEAN PLAYER TO BE CHOSEN FIRST OVERALL IN THE NHL DRAFT. THE QUEBEC NORDIQUES SELECTED HIM WITH THE TOP PICK IN 1989, AND HE JOINED THE TEAM FOR THE 1990–91 SEASON. SUNDIN SCORED 23 GOALS AS A ROOKIE THAT YEAR. THE NEXT SEASON, ▶

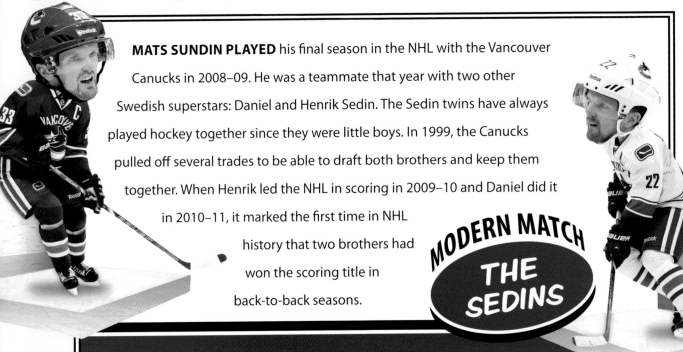

MATS SUNDIN PLAYED his final season in the NHL with the Vancouver Canucks in 2008–09. He was a teammate that year with two other Swedish superstars: Daniel and Henrik Sedin. The Sedin twins have always played hockey together since they were little boys. In 1999, the Canucks pulled off several trades to be able to draft both brothers and keep them together. When Henrik led the NHL in scoring in 2009–10 and Daniel did it in 2010–11, it marked the first time in NHL history that two brothers had won the scoring title in back-to-back seasons.

MODERN MATCH

THE SEDINS

he had 33. In his third season of 1992–93, Sundin established career highs with 47 goals, 67 assists and 114 points.

Sundin was traded to Toronto in 1994. The Maple Leafs gave up fan favorite Wendel Clark to get him, so Sundin knew he was coming into a pressure-packed situation. He responded by leading the Maple Leafs in scoring in 1994–95. Sundin would be the team's top scorer for eight straight seasons. In all, he played 13 seasons in Toronto and led the team in scoring 12 times! He holds the team record for most goals with 420 and most points with 987.

Sundin was named captain of the Maple Leafs in 1997–98. Once again, he was replacing a fan favorite — this time, Doug Gilmour. Gilmour had been a feisty player that the fans loved because he looked like he was giving 110 percent all the time. Sundin, on the other

Did You Know?

ON OCTOBER 14, 2006, MATS SUNDIN SCORED THREE GOALS, INCLUDING THE GAME-WINNER IN OVERTIME, TO REACH 500 NHL GOALS.

hand, played a calm, quiet game, and though his teammates always respected him, many fans were never as sure. Still, Sundin continued to play well. In 2001–02, he finished fourth in NHL scoring, which was the highest ranking of his career.

In all, Sundin played 18 seasons in the NHL. He never won the Stanley Cup, but he did have great success in international hockey. Sundin represented Sweden many times. He won World Championships in 1991, 1992 and 1998. In 2002, he was the top scorer at the Olympics. In 2006 he won an Olympic gold medal!

Blast FROM THE Past   JEAN RATELLE

Though one is from Sweden and the other from a small town in Quebec, there are many similarities between Mats Sundin and Jean Ratelle. Both were calm, slick centers who played a stylish game. Ratelle was a solid scorer himself, but he was even better at setting up his teammates for goals. Ratelle played for the New York Rangers and Boston Bruins between 1960 and 1981. Like Sundin, he never won the Stanley Cup, but he did enjoy success in international hockey. Ratelle played for Team Canada in 1972 when they beat Russia in the famous Summit Series.

HOCKEY HALL OF FAME: 1985

MARIO LEMIEUX

HOCKEY HALL OF FAME: 1997

HOCKEY CAME EASILY TO MARIO LEMIEUX. MAYBE TOO EASILY. WHEN HE WAS ONLY FOUR, LEMIEUX COULD DEKE OUT GOALIES THE WAY HIS NHL HEROES DID. BY THE TIME HE WAS SIX, BIG CROWDS GATHERED AT HIS GAMES. AND AT 18, LEMIEUX SET NEW RECORDS IN THE QUEBEC MAJOR JUNIOR HOCKEY LEAGUE. IN 70 GAMES THE GIFTED ▐▐▐▶

FROM THE VAULT

OH CANADA!

Mario Lemieux wore this Jersey during the 1987 Canada Cup tournament. At 6-foot-4 (193 cm) and 230 pounds (104 kg), Lemieux was blessed with size and talent. But even with all his skill, he needed to show he had the dedication to work hard and play with the best. Playing alongside Wayne Gretzky and other top talent at the Canada Cup, Lemieux showed he was ready, leading the way with 11 goals in nine games. When Gretzky set him up for the tournament-winning goal with just 1:26 remaining in the final game, it instantly became one of the greatest moments in Canadian hockey history.

goal scorer netted 133 goals and added 149 assists for a whopping 282 points! That's an average of over four points per game!

The Pittsburgh Penguins made Lemieux the first pick in the 1984 NHL Draft. That next season, 1984–85, on his first shift in his first NHL game, Lemieux raced end-to-end to score his first goal on his very first shot! Lemieux had so much talent, he didn't seem to work very hard. He topped 100 points in each of his first four NHL seasons, but people always wondered about his dedication to the game. When Lemieux finally developed the work ethic to go along with his talent, he became one of the greatest players in hockey history.

Lemieux won his first NHL scoring title in 1987–88. The next year, he won it again with a career-high 85 goals, 114 assists, and 199 points. Nobody but Wayne Gretzky has ever had a better season. In all, Lemieux led the NHL in scoring six times. He won the Hart Trophy as MVP three times and led Pittsburgh to the Stanley Cup in 1991 and 1992. Lemieux did it all despite a serious back injury. He even had to overcome cancer during his career. Lemieux retired in 1997 and soon became a part owner of the Penguins. He made a spectacular comeback with Pittsburgh three years later and also helped Team Canada win an Olympic gold medal in 2002.

Did You Know?

IN ENGLISH, MARIO LEMIEUX'S LAST NAME TRANSLATES AS "THE BEST." HE WAS CERTAINLY ONE OF THE BEST PLAYERS EVER.

Blast FROM THE Past — GILBERT PERREAULT

When the Buffalo Sabres were starting out in 1970, they made junior superstar Gilbert Perreault their very first pick in their very first NHL Draft. Like Lemieux, Perreault made the team right away. He spent his entire 17-year career in Buffalo and set every important career scoring record in Sabres history. Perreault was a wizard on the ice, skating and deking as if the puck was glued to his stick. In his early days in Buffalo, Perreault played on a line with fellow Quebec-born teammates Richard Martin and Rene Robert. They were known as "The French Connection."

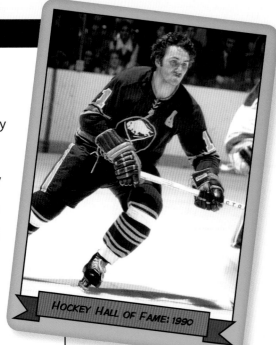

HOCKEY HALL OF FAME: 1990

GUY LAFLEUR

Hockey Hall of Fame: 1988

Plenty of rookies reach the NHL with high expectations. That's especially true for those players who are chosen first in the NHL Draft, like Guy Lafleur was in 1971. Lafleur wasn't just expected to become a superstar with the Montreal Canadiens, he was expected to replace a legend. Jean Beliveau had retired in the spring

MARTIN ST. LOUIS' career didn't start with the same expectations as Guy Lafleur's. Despite a brilliant college career, not many NHL teams noticed the 5-foot-8 (173 cm) winger. St. Louis just seemed too small. He joined the Calgary Flames in 1998, and like Lafleur, his adjustment to the NHL took time. St. Louis had a breakout season with the Tampa Bay Lightning in 2002–03. The next year he was the NHL scoring leader and a Stanley Cup champion! He won another scoring title in 2012–13. And, at 38-years old, St. Louis won a gold medal with Team Canada at the 2014 Olympics!

MODERN MATCH
MARTIN ST. LOUIS

of 1971 after leading the Canadiens to the Stanley Cup for the tenth time in his 20-year career.

Lafleur scored 29 goals as a rookie for Montreal in 1970–71, but he was still considered a disappointment. His offensive totals dropped over the next two seasons and fans began to wonder if the Canadiens had made a mistake. Players didn't have to wear helmets in the NHL during the 1970s, and before the 1974–75 season Lafleur decided to take his helmet off. He thought that if he was forced to play a little bit scared, it might help his game. Maybe it was just a coincidence, but that year, Lafleur (whose name means "the flower") finally blossomed. He was second in the NHL with 53 goals and was fourth in points with 119. For the next few years, Lafleur was the best player in the NHL. He had six straight

Did You Know?

GUY LAFLEUR IS THE CANADIENS ALL-TIME LEADER IN ASSISTS (728) AND POINTS (1,246). HIS 518 GOALS FOR MONTREAL TRAIL ONLY MAURICE RICHARD.

50-goal seasons and was named a First Team All-Star at right wing six times. He led the NHL in scoring three years in a row from 1975–76 through 1977–78 and won the Hart Trophy as MVP twice. Lafleur also helped the Canadiens win the Stanley Cup for four straight years from 1976 to 1979.

During his glory days with the Canadiens, just the sight of the speedy Lafleur, flying down the ice at the Montreal Forum with his long, blonde hair blowing in the breeze, was enough to make fans leap to their feet!

Blast FROM THE Past   JEAN BELIVEAU

Jean Beliveau was Guy Lafleur's boyhood hero. At 6-foot-3 (191 cm) and 205 pounds (93 kg), Beliveau was a big man who played hockey with power and grace. He led the NHL in goals twice and assists twice. He also won one scoring title and finished among the top ten in scoring 11 other times. Beliveau wore No. 4 for the Canadiens. When Guy Lafleur joined the team, he asked Beliveau for permission to wear his number. Knowing the pressure Lafleur would be under, Beliveau told him to pick his own number (No. 10) and make that famous by himself.

HOCKEY HALL OF FAME: 1972

JARI KURRI

Hockey Hall of Fame: 2001

Growing up in Finland, Jari Kurri didn't know very much about the NHL. Back then, NHL games weren't shown on TV in Finland, and there wasn't much coverage in Finnish newspapers. Kurri played many different sports, but when he was 15 he decided to concentrate on hockey because his friends ▶▶▶

Hockey Hall of Fame: 1998

Peter STASTNY

THE EUROPEAN CONNECTION

In the 1980s, players from Russia and Czechoslovakia (today, the Czech Republic and Slovakia) were not allowed to leave their countries to join the NHL. In the summer of 1980, Peter Stastny and his brother Anton snuck away from Czechoslovakia to play in the NHL. Another brother named Marian joined them the next year. Peter Stastny had been a top star in Europe, but he was even better in North America. He had 109 points as an NHL rookie in 1980–81 and would top 100 points six more times! During the 1980s, only Wayne Gretzky scored more points than Stastny.

were playing it. Soon, he was one of Finland's top young stars. In 1978, Kurri scored the gold medal–winning goal in overtime at the European Junior Championship. Two years later, in 1980, Kurri helped Finland win a silver medal at the World Junior Championship. His performance there earned him a spot on the 1980 Finnish Olympic team.

The Edmonton Oilers choose Kurri in the fourth round of the 1980 NHL Draft. During the 1980–81 season, he began playing right wing on a line with Wayne Gretzky. Kurri was a good defensive forward, but he also had a very accurate shot. He began piling up points as he cashed in the perfect passes he got from Gretzky. Kurri had his first 50-goal season in 1983–84 and helped Edmonton win the Stanley Cup that year. It was the first of five Stanley Cup victories for the Oilers over a seven-year stretch!

Kurri scored a career-high 71 goals in 1984–85. Gretzky led the NHL with 73 that season, making him and Kurri the only two teammates in league history to top 70 goals! When the Oilers won the Stanley Cup that season, Kurri tied an NHL record with 19 goals in the playoffs. He led the NHL with 68 goals in 1985–86.

Kurri was traded by Edmonton in 1990, and he retired in 1998. At the time, his 601 career goals were the most by a player from Europe.

Did You Know?

JARI KURRI HAD 12 GOALS IN THE 1985 CONFERENCE FINALS TO SET A PLAYOFF RECORD FOR THE MOST GOALS IN A SINGLE SERIES. THE RECORD HAS NEVER BEEN BROKEN.

MODERN MATCH
TEEMU SELANNE

HARDLY ANYONE HAD heard of Teemu Selanne when the Winnipeg Jets made him their first choice during the 1988 NHL Draft. Selanne continued to play in Finland for the next four years. When he finally joined the Jets in 1992–93, it was worth the wait. Selanne shattered the rookie scoring record with 76 goals that year! He also added 56 assists for 132 points. His blazing speed and scoring skill earned him the nickname "The Finnish Flash." Selanne went on to lead the NHL in goals two more times and has surpassed Jari Kurri as the all-time scoring leader from Finland.

JOE SAKIC

Hockey Hall of Fame: 2012

JOE SAKIC PLAYED 20 NHL SEASONS, ALL WITH THE SAME ORGANIZATION BUT IN TWO DIFFERENT CITIES. HE BEGAN HIS CAREER IN 1988–89 WITH THE QUEBEC NORDIQUES. AFTER SEVEN SEASONS, THE NORDIQUES MOVED TO DENVER AND BECAME THE COLORADO AVALANCHE.

JOHN TAVARES WAS ready to play junior hockey when he was only 14 years old. The rules in the Ontario Hockey League (OHL) said a player had to be 15 to be drafted, but a new rule was passed for Tavares. In his first year in the OHL in 2005–06, Tavares was named rookie of the year. He went on to set a league scoring record with 215 goals in his four-year junior career. In 2009, the New York Islanders chose Tavares first in the NHL Draft. He's gone on to become one of the NHL's top young stars. In 2014 Tavares won an Olympic gold medal with Team Canada!

MODERN MATCH
JOHN TAVARES

He spent 13 more years with the team there. Sakic was a quiet superstar who liked to let his skill speak for itself. It meant he didn't always get the attention he deserved, but when he retired in 2009, he was one of just seven players in NHL history with over 600 goals and more than 1,000 assists.

Sakic was only four years old when he decided he wanted to make hockey his career. Lots of children say they want to be hockey stars, but not very many ever make it. Sakic clearly had the talent and the dedication to keep at it.

At 17, he was the rookie of the year in the Western Hockey League. The next season, he was the league's top scorer. A year after that, he was playing in the NHL.

In just his second season of 1989–90, Sakic cracked the top 10 in NHL scoring. It was the first of ten times he would do that. It was also his first of six seasons with 100-or-more points. Still, the Nordiques struggled just to make the playoffs each year. Then, when the team moved to Colorado in 1995–96, success came instantly. Sakic set career highs with 69 assists and 120 points that season and led Colorado to the Stanley Cup. Five years later, Sakic scored a career-high 54 goals and led Colorado to the Stanley Cup again! Sakic was the playoff MVP in 1996. In 2001, he won the Hart Trophy as the most valuable player in the whole league.

Did You Know?

JOE SAKIC HOLDS THE ALL-TIME NHL RECORD FOR THE MOST PLAYOFF OVERTIME GOALS WITH EIGHT IN HIS CAREER.

Blast FROM THE Past STAN MIKITA

Stan Mikita spent his entire 22-year career with the Chicago Black Hawks from 1958 to 1980. Early in his career, Mikita got lots of penalties. When he realized he was setting a bad example for his daughter, he decided to clean up his game. Mikita had already led the NHL in scoring twice. Then, in 1966–67, he became the first player to win three major awards in one season. In addition to the Art Ross Trophy for scoring and the Hart Trophy as MVP, he also won the Lady Byng Trophy for sportsmanship. He won all three trophies again in 1967–68.

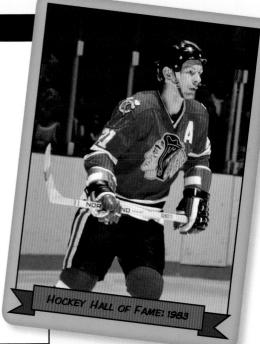

HOCKEY HALL OF FAME: 1983

MARK MESSIER

Hockey Hall of Fame: 2007

Doug Messier was a minor-pro defenseman in the 1960s. He was good, but never made the NHL. He taught his son Mark about the kind of hard work it took to make it as a pro hockey player. Mark not only made the NHL, but he had one of the greatest careers in NHL history! His teammates always saw how hard he worked to ▶

FROM THE VAULT

THE CAPTAIN'S JERSEY

Mark Messier wore this jersey during Oilers' home games in the 1990 Stanley Cup Final. Most people predicted a tight battle between Edmonton and Boston that year, but the Oilers beat the Bruins in five games. It was their fifth Stanley Cup victory in seven years, but their only one without Wayne Gretzky. Game 1 in the 1990 series went until 15:13 of triple overtime before the Oilers finally won it. It's the longest game in the history of the Stanley Cup Final.

succeed, and it made them work harder too. That's what made Messier such a great leader.

Mark was a late bloomer, but in 1982–83, his fourth professional season, he had a breakout year for the Edmonton Oilers and scored 50 goals. When the Oilers won the Stanley Cup for the first time in 1983–84, Messier was the playoff MVP. Wayne Gretzky was the biggest star on those Edmonton teams, but when he was traded after their fourth Stanley Cup victory in 1987–88, Messier was named captain. The Oilers won the Stanley Cup again (Messier's fifth) in 1989–90. That year Messier notched 84 assists and 129 points and won the Hart Trophy as the NHL's most valuable player.

At the start of the 1991–92 season, Messier was traded to the New York

Did You Know?

MARK MESSIER PLAYED 1,756 GAMES IN HIS CAREER AND HAD 1,881 POINTS. BOTH TOTALS RANK SECOND IN NHL HISTORY.

Rangers. He won the Hart Trophy that season too, but what Ranger fans really wanted was the Stanley Cup. Their team hadn't won it since 1940. In 1993–94, Messier delivered the long-awaited victory. He scored the winning goal in Game 7 of the Final and became the only player in NHL history to captain two different teams to the Stanley Cup!

In his career, Messier topped 100 points six times. He played both left wing and center and is the only player in NHL history to be selected a First Team All-Star at both positions.

JAROME IGINLA STARRED with the Calgary Flames from 1996 to 2013. Like Messier, he is a leader known for his hard work. By his third season in Calgary, Iginla was the team's top goal scorer. He led the team again ten times in the next 12 years! Iginla was captain of the Flames for nine years, and led them all the way to Game 7 of the Stanley Cup Final in 2003–04, although Calgary didn't win. He led the team in points every season from 2000–01 to 2011–12, and in 2001–02 Iginla led the NHL with 52 goals and 96 points.

MODERN MATCH

JAROME IGINLA

BOBBY CLARKE

Hockey Hall of Fame: 1987

BOBBY CLARKE WON THREE LEAGUE SCORING TITLES IN A ROW PLAYING JUNIOR HOCKEY IN HIS HOMETOWN OF FLIN FLON, MANITOBA. HE SHOULD HAVE BEEN ONE OF THE TOP CHOICES IN THE 1969 NHL DRAFT. INSTEAD, IT TOOK UNTIL THE SECOND ROUND BEFORE THE PHILADELPHIA FLYERS PICKED HIM. CLARKE HAD DIABETES, AND TEAMS WERE AFRAID HE ▐▐▐➤

Dynamite Linemates

BILL BARBER (HHOF: 1990)

Bill Barber played left wing and center as a junior with the Kitchener Rangers. When Philadelphia selected him with the seventh pick in the 1972 NHL Draft, they decided to play him at left wing on a line with Bobby Clarke. Barber had good hands and an excellent shot. He was a great match for Clarke's passing skills and led all rookies in 1972–73 with 30 goals. Barber scored a career-high 50 goals in 1975–76. His 420 goals during 12 years with the Flyers remain a team record.

wouldn't be strong enough to play in the NHL. But he never let the disease get in his way. Clarke always took proper care of himself, and he had the drive and determination needed to succeed.

The NHL had expanded in size from six to 12 teams in 1967. The Flyers were one of the six new teams, and Bobby Clarke quickly became their leader. He was named team captain in 1972, and the Flyers built a tough team, known as the "Broad Street Bullies," around Clarke and his rough and tumble game. Philadelphia had plenty of fighters and Clarke and the Bullies took lots of penalties, but they had a lot of skill too. During the 1972–73 season, Clarke became the first player from a 1967 expansion team to score 100 points. He finished with 104, good for second in scoring behind Phil Esposito. More importantly, Clarke won his first Hart Trophy as NHL MVP that year. The Flyers became the first expansion team to win the Stanley Cup when they won back-to-back championships in 1973–74 and 1974–75. Clarke won his second Hart Trophy in 1974–75, and the next year set a career high with 119 points, winning his third MVP award!

Clarke spent his entire playing career with Philadelphia, and he still holds Flyers team records for the most seasons (15), the most games (1,144), the most assists (852) and the most points (1,210).

Did You Know?

BOBBY CLARKE WAS A STRONG TWO-WAY PLAYER. HE WON THE SELKE TROPHY AS THE NHL'S BEST DEFENSIVE FORWARD IN 1982–83.

Blast FROM THE Past   HARRY BROADBENT (HHOF: 1962)

Harry "Punch" Broadbent was a high-scoring star who was as tough as he was talented. Broadbent could deke around his opponents, but sometimes he would just skate right over them! Broadbent's pro career, which included time in Montreal and New York, began with the Ottawa Senators in 1912. His best season came in 1921–22. That year, he led the NHL with 32 goals and 46 points in just 24 games played. Broadbent set a record that season that still stands by scoring at least one goal in 16 consecutive games!

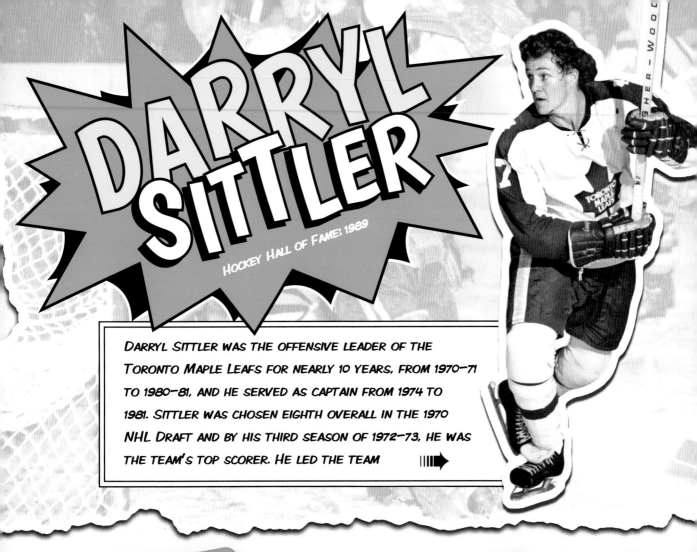

DARRYL SITTLER

Hockey Hall of Fame: 1989

DARRYL SITTLER WAS THE OFFENSIVE LEADER OF THE TORONTO MAPLE LEAFS FOR NEARLY 10 YEARS, FROM 1970-71 TO 1980-81, AND HE SERVED AS CAPTAIN FROM 1974 TO 1981. SITTLER WAS CHOSEN EIGHTH OVERALL IN THE 1970 NHL DRAFT AND BY HIS THIRD SEASON OF 1972-73, HE WAS THE TEAM'S TOP SCORER. HE LED THE TEAM ▮▮▮▶

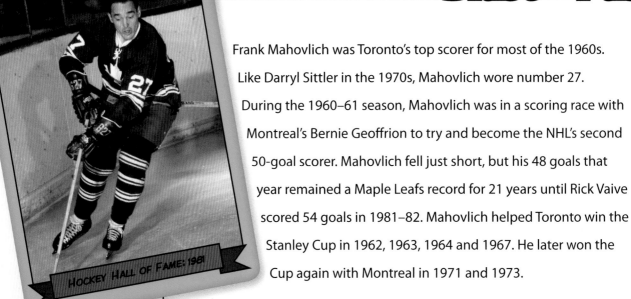

FRANK MAHOVLICH

Blast FROM THE Past

Frank Mahovlich was Toronto's top scorer for most of the 1960s. Like Darryl Sittler in the 1970s, Mahovlich wore number 27. During the 1960–61 season, Mahovlich was in a scoring race with Montreal's Bernie Geoffrion to try and become the NHL's second 50-goal scorer. Mahovlich fell just short, but his 48 goals that year remained a Maple Leafs record for 21 years until Rick Vaive scored 54 goals in 1981–82. Mahovlich helped Toronto win the Stanley Cup in 1962, 1963, 1964 and 1967. He later won the Cup again with Montreal in 1971 and 1973.

Hockey Hall of Fame: 1981

in scoring six more times and became the first player in Maple Leafs history to hit the 100-point mark. But it is what he did on February 7, 1976, that still has hockey fans talking today.

Toronto was facing Boston that night. The Bruins had won seven in a row, but the Maple Leafs beat them badly and Sittler set a record that has never been broken. He had 10 points in a single game! Midway through the first period, Sittler set up a pair of goals to put Toronto ahead 2–0. He had two more assists and scored three goals of his own in the second period for seven points. The NHL record was eight, and Sittler tied it with his fourth goal of the night 44 seconds into the third period. He broke the record with his fifth goal midway through the third period, then added one more a little bit later. Sittler finished the night with six goals and four assists and Toronto won the game 11–4!

Sittler had another big night two months later. On April 22, 1976, he tied an NHL playoff record with five goals in one game. His best season, however, came in 1977–78 when Sittler set career highs with 45 goals, 72 assists and 117 points. His third-place finish in the scoring race that year marked the first time since the 1945–46 season that a Toronto player had finished as a top-three scorer!

Did You Know?

DARRYL SITTLER SCORED THE WINNING GOAL IN OVERTIME WHEN TEAM CANADA WON THE FIRST CANADA CUP TOURNAMENT IN 1976.

Dynamite Linemates

LANNY MCDONALD (HHOF: 1992)

Lanny McDonald was a junior scoring star in Medicine Hat, Alberta, when Toronto chose him fourth overall in 1973. In his third season with Toronto in 1975–76, the right winger was placed on a line with center Darryl Sittler, and he took off! McDonald jumped from 44 points to 93 that season, and topped 40 goals in each of the next three years. Toronto traded McDonald midway through the 1979–80 season. Two years later, he wound up in Calgary. During the 1982–83 season, McDonald set a Flames record that still stands, by scoring 66 goals!

STEVE YZERMAN

Hockey Hall of Fame: 2009

STEVE YZERMAN LOVED HOCKEY AS A BOY. THE WALLS IN HIS ROOM WERE COVERED WITH POSTERS OF PLAYERS FROM ALL GENERATIONS. YZERMAN LEARNED TO SKATE ON A LAKE NEAR HIS HOMETOWN OF CRANBROOK, BRITISH COLUMBIA. HE BEGAN PLAYING HOCKEY AFTER THE FAMILY MOVED TO THE OTTAWA SUBURB OF NEPEAN, ONTARIO. WHEN HE WAS 18, THE DETROIT RED WINGS CHOSE YZERMAN FOURTH ▸

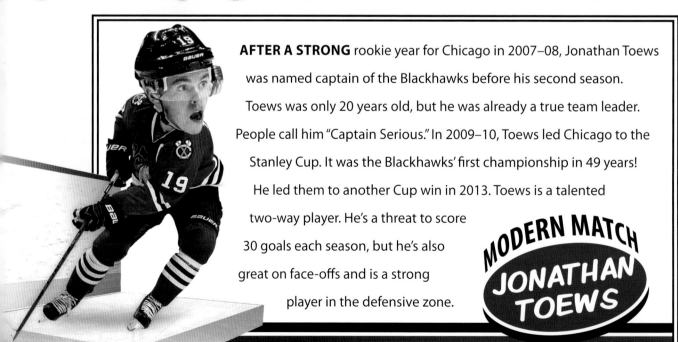

AFTER A STRONG rookie year for Chicago in 2007–08, Jonathan Toews was named captain of the Blackhawks before his second season. Toews was only 20 years old, but he was already a true team leader. People call him "Captain Serious." In 2009–10, Toews led Chicago to the Stanley Cup. It was the Blackhawks' first championship in 49 years! He led them to another Cup win in 2013. Toews is a talented two-way player. He's a threat to score 30 goals each season, but he's also great on face-offs and is a strong player in the defensive zone.

MODERN MATCH: JONATHAN TOEWS

overall in the 1983 NHL Draft. He made the team that year and went on to play 22 seasons for Detroit — that's a long time!

In 1983–84, the 18-year-old Yzerman set Red Wings rookie records with 39 goals and 87 points. He also became the youngest player to play in the NHL All-Star Game. By the time he was 21 he was Detroit's captain, and when he was 22, in 1987–88, Yzerman scored 50 goals and had 102 points. What's more impressive is that he scored all those points in only 64 games! It was the first of six straight seasons that Yzerman registered 100 points or more. Still, when Scotty Bowman became the Red Wings coach in 1993–94, he demanded that the slick scorer improve his defensive skills. Yzerman eventually became one of the league's best defensive forwards, and his two-way play helped Detroit win the

Did You Know?

STEVE YZERMAN WON AN OLYMPIC GOLD MEDAL FOR CANADA AS A PLAYER IN 2002 AND AS GENERAL MANAGER IN 2010 AND 2014.

Stanley Cup in 1997. It was the first time the Red Wings had won it in 42 years! Yzerman captained Detroit to Cup wins again in 1998 and 2002.

Injuries slowed him down in his later years, but when Yzerman retired in 2006, he had scored 692 goals. His 1,063 assists broke the team record of 1,023 previously held by Gordie Howe. By then, Yzerman had been captain of the Red Wings for 20 years. That's by far the longest time that any player has worn the "C" in NHL history!

MVP JERSEY

Steve Yzerman wore this jersey for Detroit during the 1988–89 season. That year, Yzerman set Red Wings records with 65 goals, 90 assists and 155 points. Not only was it the greatest offensive season in team history, it was one of the greatest in NHL history too. Only Wayne Gretzky and Mario Lemieux have ever scored more points in a single season than Yzerman did that year. Sportswriters voted for Wayne Gretzky as the winner of the Hart Trophy as NHL MVP that season, but when the players cast their own votes for MVP, they chose Yzerman.

FROM THE VAULT

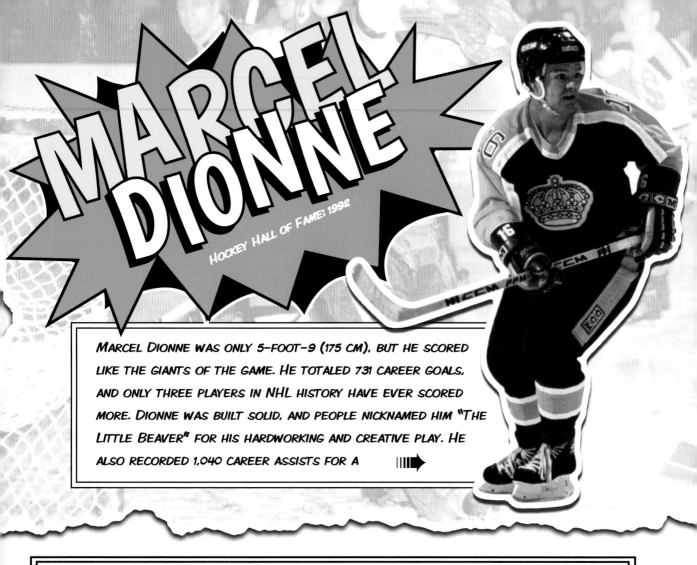

MARCEL DIONNE

HOCKEY HALL OF FAME: 1992

MARCEL DIONNE WAS ONLY 5-FOOT-9 (175 CM), BUT HE SCORED LIKE THE GIANTS OF THE GAME. HE TOTALED 731 CAREER GOALS, AND ONLY THREE PLAYERS IN NHL HISTORY HAVE EVER SCORED MORE. DIONNE WAS BUILT SOLID, AND PEOPLE NICKNAMED HIM "THE LITTLE BEAVER" FOR HIS HARDWORKING AND CREATIVE PLAY. HE ALSO RECORDED 1,040 CAREER ASSISTS FOR A

MODERN MATCH
ANZE KOPITAR

ANZE KOPITAR IS the first NHL player from the Eastern European country of Slovenia. There was no league good enough to match his skill level in Slovenia, so when Kopitar was 16 he left home to play junior hockey in Sweden. When he was 18, Los Angeles made him the 11th player chosen in the 2005 NHL Draft. He joined the Kings in 2006–07 and scored two goals in his very first NHL game! Kopitar has been the Kings' top offensive player ever since. In 2011, he helped Los Angeles win the Stanley Cup for the first time.

combined total of 1,771 points, which is fifth best in NHL history. Yet, unlike a giant, Marcel Dionne always seemed to be playing in someone else's shadow.

As a junior player before he reached the NHL, Dionne and Guy Lafleur were big rivals. In fact, there were some people with the Montreal Canadiens who wanted Dionne instead of Lafleur. Ultimately, the Canadiens chose Lafleur with the top pick in 1971, and Dionne went to Detroit with the second choice. He set a new rookie record with 77 points that season, but when the time came to hand out the Calder Trophy, Canadiens goalie Ken Dryden was named rookie of the year.

Dionne finished third in NHL scoring with 121 points in 1974–75, but after that season he left Detroit for Los Angeles. The Kings weren't very popular then, so even though Dionne topped 50 goals six times and 100 points on seven more occasions, someone else usually won the NHL's top awards. Even when Dionne did win the NHL scoring title in 1979–80, his victory was unusual. He and Wayne Gretzky both finished the season with 139 points, but Dionne was given the Art Ross Trophy because he'd scored 53 goals to Gretzky's 51. Even so, it was Gretzky who was named league MVP. Dionne's teams never won a championship either, making him probably the best player in NHL history to never get his name on the Stanley Cup.

Did You Know?

IN 1980–81, EACH PLAYER ON THE KINGS' TRIPLE CROWN LINE OF MARCEL DIONNE, CHARLIE SIMMER AND DAVE TAYLOR TOPPED 100 POINTS.

Blast FROM THE Past — CY DENNENY (HHOF: 1959)

Cy Denneny didn't look like an athlete. He was kind of pudgy. He wasn't a great skater either, but Denneny had a hard, accurate shot. Some people even said he could make the puck curve when he shot it. Like Dionne, Denneny was a star player, but it often seemed that someone else was a little bit better. During the NHL's first season of 1917–18, Denneny had a career-high 36 goals in just 20 games but Joe Malone led the league with 44. Denneny won the scoring title in 1923–24, but he finished second five times.

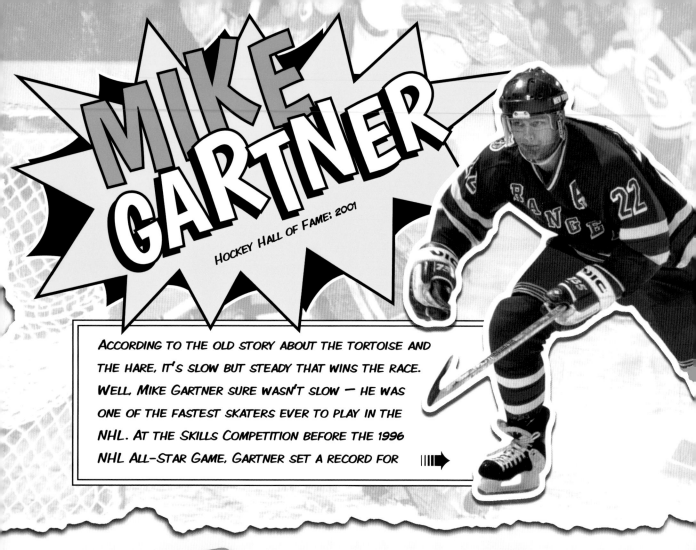

MIKE GARTNER

Hockey Hall of Fame: 2001

According to the old story about the tortoise and the hare, it's slow but steady that wins the race. Well, Mike Gartner sure wasn't slow — he was one of the fastest skaters ever to play in the NHL. At the Skills Competition before the 1996 NHL All-Star Game, Gartner set a record for ▐▐▶

YVON COURNOYER — Blast FROM THE Past

Hockey Hall of Fame: 1982

Yvon Cournoyer played in the NHL from 1963 to 1979. He spent his whole career with the Montreal Canadiens. In those 16 years, he got his name on the Stanley Cup 10 times! Cournoyer was only 5-foot-7 (170 cm), but he was fast. He was nicknamed "The Roadrunner" after the speedy cartoon bird. Cournoyer's speed allowed him to swoop in on loose pucks, and his skill on his skates made it hard for the bigger players to hit him. Cournoyer had 40 goals or more four times in his career. He ranked among the NHL's top goal scorers six times.

the fastest lap around the rink. He made it all the way around the ice in just 13.386 seconds. His record wasn't broken for 16 years! So, Gartner wasn't slow, but he sure was steady. In fact, he may have been the most consistent scorer in hockey history.

Mike Gartner began his career in the World Hockey Association (WHA) in 1978–79. That year, he was the runner-up to Wayne Gretzky for the WHA rookie of the year. The next season, Gartner entered the NHL with the Washington Capitals. He scored 36 goals to set a Washington rookie record that was finally broken by Alex Ovechkin in 2005–06. For Gartner, it was the first of 15 straight seasons in which he scored at least 30 goals. That's a record that's only been matched once, by Jaromir Jagr. Gartner's streak was finally snapped by a strike-shortened season in 1994–95. He only

got to play in 38 games that year. The next season, he bounced back with 35 goals for the Toronto Maple Leafs. In all, Gartner scored 30 goals or more 17 times in his 19-year career. That's a record that no one has beaten! Gartner only scored 50 goals once, but he was his team's top goal-scorer nine times. He never led the league, but with his steady performance year after year, Gartner was just the fifth player in NHL history to score more than 700 goals. He had 708 when he retired in 1998.

MIKE'S LID

Mike Gartner wore this helmet during his days with the Washington Capitals. Back then, it was rare for players to wear a visor. Gartner was one of the first big stars to do so. He put it on after he was hit in the eye with a puck during the 1982–83 season. "The doctors have told me I have to wear it," Gartner later explained. "So I do. I wouldn't think of going out there without my pants or my shoulder pads...I have to look at the shield the same way. It's part of my equipment."

FROM THE VAULT

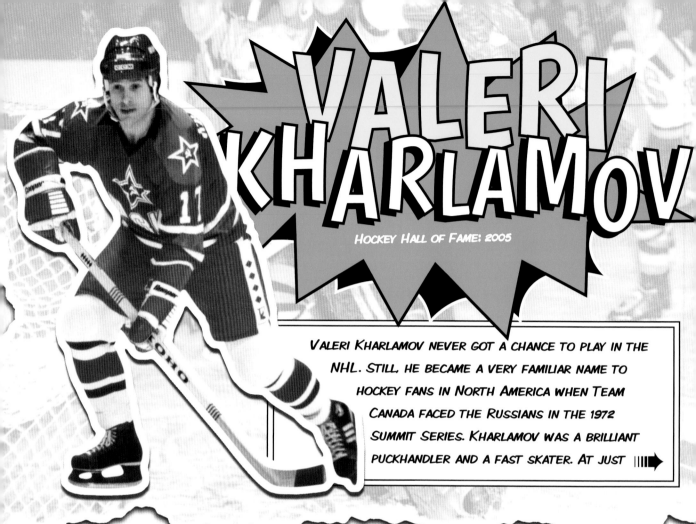

VALERI KHARLAMOV

HOCKEY HALL OF FAME: 2005

VALERI KHARLAMOV NEVER GOT A CHANCE TO PLAY IN THE NHL. STILL, HE BECAME A VERY FAMILIAR NAME TO HOCKEY FANS IN NORTH AMERICA WHEN TEAM CANADA FACED THE RUSSIANS IN THE 1972 SUMMIT SERIES. KHARLAMOV WAS A BRILLIANT PUCKHANDLER AND A FAST SKATER. AT JUST ▮▮▶

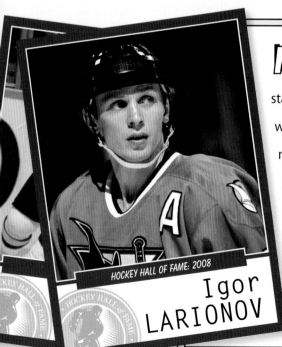

HOCKEY HALL OF FAME: 2008

Igor LARIONOV

NEXT GENERATION

Igor Larionov was a top star in Russia during the 1980s. He centered the famous KLM Line with Vladimir Krutov and Sergei Makarov. When Larionov was nearly 29 years old, Russian players were finally allowed into the NHL. He joined the Vancouver Canucks for the 1989–90 season. Later, he played in San Jose, Florida and New Jersey. His best years in the NHL came with Detroit. The Red Wings had another Russian veteran, Slava Fetisov. They also had several young Russian stars. Larionov fit in right away and helped Detroit win the Stanley Cup in 1997, 1998 and 2002.

5-foot-8 (172 cm) and 165 pounds (73 kg), he wasn't very big, but he was strong. He was never afraid to go one-on-one against the world's toughest defensemen.

Kharlamov's hockey talent was obvious when he was just a boy. At 14, he became part of the top club in Russia — Moscow's Central Red Army. By the time he was 20 in 1968, he was playing with the Red Army's best team in the top Russian league.

In 1972, Russia won gold at the Winter Olympics. A few months later, the Russian team played the top Canadian stars from the NHL in a special series of eight exhibition games. Russia had dominated the Olympics and the World Championships for years, but many said it was because NHL players weren't allowed to participate. So, most people in Canada expected the NHL stars to win the Summit Series. They were certainly shocked when Kharlamov scored two goals to lead Russia to a 7–3 win in game one. The series went right down to

the wire before Team Canada won it in the final seconds of the final game.

Kharlamov played in 11 World Championships during his career, winning a medal every time, including eight golds, two silvers and one bronze. He also won two golds and one silver in three tries at the Olympics. In regular-season play, Kharlamov and the Red Army won 11 league championships. He had 293 goals and 509 points in 436 games. Sadly, Kharlamov was killed in a car accident in 1981.

Did You Know?

VALERI KHARLAMOV WAS NAMED AN ALL-STAR AT THE WORLD CHAMPIONSHIP TOURNAMENT IN 1972, 1973, 1975 AND 1976.

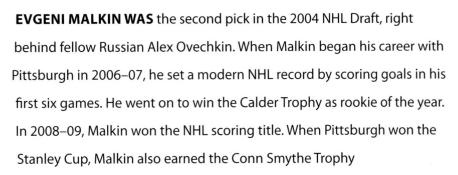

EVGENI MALKIN WAS the second pick in the 2004 NHL Draft, right behind fellow Russian Alex Ovechkin. When Malkin began his career with Pittsburgh in 2006–07, he set a modern NHL record by scoring goals in his first six games. He went on to win the Calder Trophy as rookie of the year. In 2008–09, Malkin won the NHL scoring title. When Pittsburgh won the Stanley Cup, Malkin also earned the Conn Smythe Trophy as playoff MVP. He won another scoring title in 2011–12. Malkin wears No. 71 for Pittsburgh in tribute to Valeri Kharlamov, whose number was 17.

MODERN MATCH
EVGENI MALKIN

RON FRANCIS

Hockey Hall of Fame: 2007

RON FRANCIS PLAYED 23 SEASONS IN THE NHL FROM 1981 TO 2004. HE WAS A CONSISTENT SCORER WHO HAD 549 CAREER GOALS. AND WHILE HE NEVER HAD MORE THAN 32 GOALS IN HIS BEST YEAR, HE SCORED 20-PLUS GOALS 20 TIMES! ONLY GORDIE HOWE HAS MORE 20-GOAL SEASONS THAN THAT. STILL, SCORING GOALS WASN'T ▐▐▐▶

MODERN MATCH
JOE THORNTON

BIG THINGS WERE expected in Boston when the Bruins chose Joe Thornton first overall in the 1997 NHL Draft. He developed slowly, but by 2002–03 he was named team captain and topped 100 points for the first time. Even so, the Bruins traded Thornton to the Sharks early in 2005–06. Splitting that season between Boston and San Jose, Thornton led the league with 96 assists. He also won the Art Ross Trophy as NHL scoring leader with 125 points. Thornton led the league in assists again in 2006–07 and 2007–08. He is still one of the NHL's best playmakers.

what Francis was known for. He was a playmaker and a defensive forward. Francis ranked among the NHL's top 10 in assists 12 times and led the league twice. By the end of his career, Francis had accumulated 1,249 assists. That ranks him second all-time behind only Wayne Gretzky. He ranks third all-time in games played with 1,731 and fourth in points with 1,798.

Francis began his career with the Hartford Whalers. He was their first choice, fourth overall, in the 1981 NHL Draft and joined the team partway through the 1981–82 season. Francis quickly became one of Hartford's top players, and in his fourth season he was named captain. Soon, the Whalers were a consistent playoff team, though they rarely managed to win even a single round. Late in the 1990–91 season, Francis was traded to Pittsburgh. He took his game to a whole new level

with the Penguins. Centering the team's second line, behind Mario Lemieux and Jaromir Jagr, Francis helped Pittsburgh win the Stanley Cup that year. They won it again in 1991–92. He remained in Pittsburgh until 1998. During the 1997–98 season, Francis's old team from Hartford moved to Carolina and became the Hurricanes. Francis rejoined the team in 1998–99. In all, he spent 16 seasons with the Whalers/Hurricanes. He holds the franchise records for most games (1,186), most goals (382), most assists (793) and most points (1,175).

Blast FROM THE Past   FRANK BOUCHER (HHOF: 1958)

In hockey's early days, passing the puck forward was against the rules. For the 1929–30 season, the NHL finally allowed forward passing in every zone. Before then, no one had ever had more than 18 assists in a season. But that year, Frank Boucher doubled the NHL record to 36 assists. Boucher centered high-scoring brothers Bill and Bun Cook on the New York Rangers' top line. Between 1926–27 and 1934–35, Boucher led the NHL in assists three times and finished second four times. He also won the Lady Byng Trophy for sportsmanship a record seven times!

INDEX

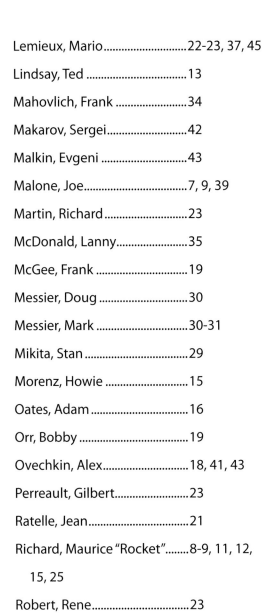

PHOTO CREDITS

T=Top, B= Bottom, BL=Bottom left, BR=Bottom right,

All illustrations © George Todorovic

Hockey Hall of Fame

Graphic Artists/HHOF 5 (Hull, Clarke), 14T, 32T, 32B, 34T, 34B; Paul Bereswill/HHOF 6T, 10T, 22T, 26T, 38T, 40T; Doug MacLellan/HHOF 5 (Yzerman), 16B, 36T; Matthew Manor/HHOF 12B, 22B, 41B; Mecca/HHOF 10BR; O-Pee-Chee/HHOF 23B; Portnoy/HHOF 10BL, 18T, 21B, 23B, 29B, 35B, 40B; Chris Relke/HHOF 8B, 42B; Hal Roth/HHOF 17B, 30B, 37B; Dave Sandford/HHOF 5 (Sundin, Messier), 16T, 20T, 28T, 30T, 44T; Bob Shaver/HHOF 24T; Le Studio du Hockey/HHOF 8T, 25B; Imperial Oil–Turofsky/HHOF 12T, 13BL, 13BR. All images used for the cover are listed above as they appear in the book.

Icon Sports Images

Robin Alam/Icon SMI 5(Toews), 36B; Dustin Bradford/Icon SMI 14B; Rich Graessle/Icon SMI 24B, 28B; Kathleen Hinkel/Icon SMI 20BL; Rich Kane/Icon SMI 20BR; Fred Kfoury/Icon SMI 31B; Jeanine Leech/Icon SMI 5 (Crosby), 5 (Ovechkin), 6B, 11B, 18B, 43B; Mark LoMoglio/Icon SMI 38B; Ric Tapia/Icon SMI 44; Cliff Welch/Icon SMI 27B.

Getty Images

Melchior DiGiacomo/Getty Images 42T.